Water Play

Written by
Cally Chambers

Original activities by
Kay Davies and Wendy Oldfield

Photography by
Zul Mukhida

Wayland

Science Busy Books

Glue and Paint Pots
Odds and Ends
Toys and Models
Water Play

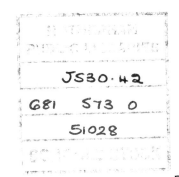

First published in 1992 by Wayland (Publishers) Ltd
61 Western Road, Hove, East Sussex, BN3 1JD, England

© Copyright 1992 Wayland (Publishers) Ltd

Consultant: **Graham Peacock**, Senior Lecturer, Centre for Science
    Education, Sheffield City Polytechnic

British Library Cataloguing in Publication Data
Chambers, Cally
    Water play.—(Science Busy Books)
    I. Title   II. Davies, Kay, *1946—*
    III. Oldfield, Wendy   IV. Series
    553.7

HARDBACK ISBN 0 7502 0351 X

PAPERBACK ISBN 0 7502 0593 8

Typeset by Dorchester Typesetting Group Ltd
Printed and bound in Belgium by Casterman S. A.

In this book you will find:

Topic Key

This key shows you where to find activities that introduce common science topics.

Air
4, 5, 6

Growth
14

Capacity and volume
16

Hot and cold
15

Colour and light
9, 12

Metals
18, 19

Comparing materials
8, 9, 13

Sound
13

Displacement
6, 7

Structures
5, 10, 11

Floating and sinking
4, 5, 6, 7, 8, 9, 10, 11

Waste
17

Annie holds the empty bottle under the water.

But it isn't really empty at all. It is full of air.

Bubbles of air escape from the bottle. It fills up with water.

The bubbles float up to the surface of the water.

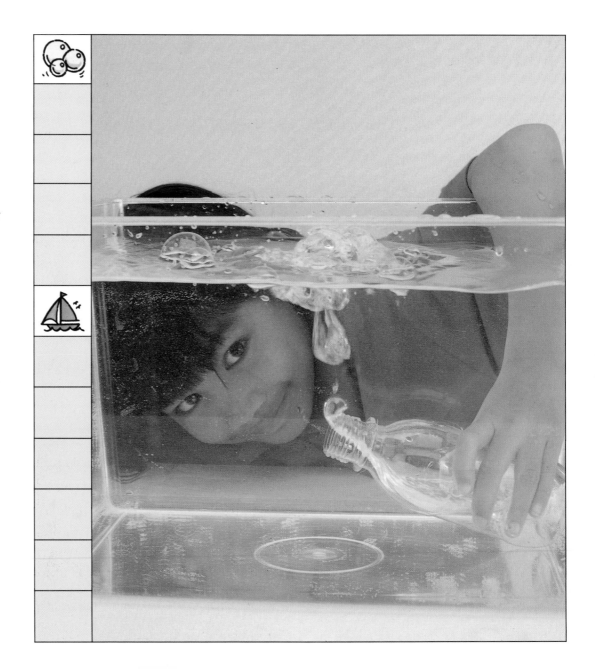

Kelly holds a large sponge under water.

Lots of tiny bubbles escape from the sponge. They float to the surface.

She tries to squeeze it really tight to get every last bubble out.

What will happen when she takes the sponge out of the water?

Alex has blown up a big balloon.

He has to try very hard to push the balloon under water.

It wants to stay on top of the water.

What is the balloon full of?

Emily lifts a solid brick into the tank full of water.

Water spills out.

The brick has pushed the water out of the way.

Watch what happens when you use half a tank of water to do this.

Use a pen to mark the water-level on the tank first.

Peter is testing objects that he thinks will float in water.

How many do you recognize?

Was he wrong about any of them?

Make a collection of objects you would like to test.

Robert has found lots of things that sink in water.

How many of these can you spot:

- a metal spoon?
- glass marbles?
- plastic buttons?
- small stones?

When Robert drops objects into the tank, they look different.

What do you notice if you look at things in a jar of water?

Thomas has made some cork boats.

The boats float better with plasticine weights underneath them.

The weights stop the boats rolling over.

Can you make some cork boats using different plasticine weights?

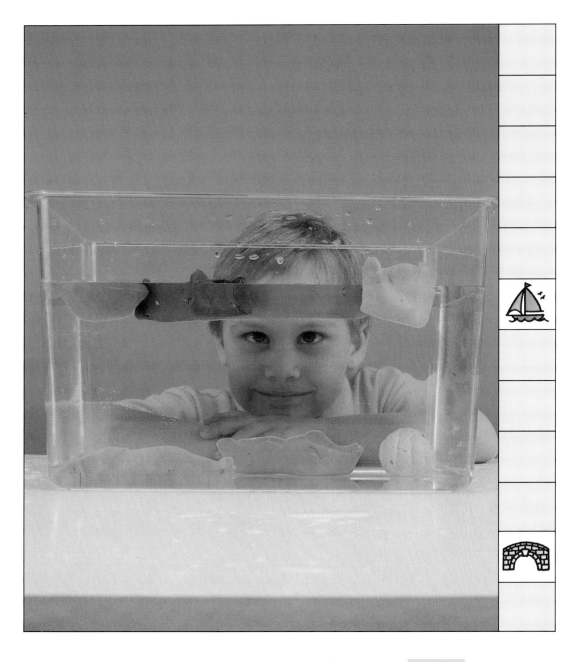

A ball of plasticine won't float by itself.

Tim has made boat shapes from plasticine.

Some are round and some are long.

Some have high sides and some have low sides.

Can you make a plasticine boat that floats well?

Sam has mixed some paints in water.

He has dropped a little blue paint in the jar. Then he has added a few drops of red.

What colour do they make when they mix?

What colour do you get when you mix blue and yellow?

Fipe and James are practising sound effects for a play.

Fipe gently rolls a box with small stones in it.

James blows through straws into a jar of water.

They make a sound like waves splashing on a pebbly beach.

Can you make some sound effects?

All living things need water to grow.

Natasha has been growing mustard.

She filled two jars with paper and sprinkled some seeds on top.

She watered one jar and left the other dry.

Which jar did she water? Which jar did she leave dry?

We can feel the difference between hot and cold water.

Rachael is using a thermometer to measure the difference exactly.

The jar of ice cubes is very cold and the temperature is low.

She puts the thermometer in a jar of warm water.

The temperature shoots right up.

Stacey has collected lots of bottles. They are all different sizes and shapes.

How many small bottles full of water will it take to fill the brown bottle?

Stacey guesses three and a half. She finds that she is right.

Collect four bottles. Put them in order of size by looking at them. How can you test if you are right?

The bucket is full of muddy water.

Stanley and Fifi want to make it clean again.

Their teacher has cut the bottom off a large plastic bottle. They have half filled it with small stones.

Fifi pours the dirty water into the home-made filter.

This takes all the large pieces of dirt out of the water.

Fifi put a large iron nail in a jar of water.

Then she left the jar for a few days.

Now the nail is covered in a layer of red rust.

Iron is a kind of metal.

Iron things always go rusty in water.

Fifi wants to find out what happens to other metals in water.

She puts metal objects into jam jars.

After a few days, she looks at them.

Some metals don't change in water.

How many rusty things can you see in this picture?

Helpful Hints for Parents and Teachers

Play is an important learning method at primary level. This is because it allows children to explore and experience for themselves. It encourages them to ask questions and experiment to find their own answers. In small groups, children bounce ideas off each other and extend each other's learning.

Most activities in this book involve methods of observation and recording that do not rely on writing skills. Because of this, the activities are especially useful for nursery and infant children.

Page 4 We can't see air but it is all around us. It is lighter than water and so floats up to the surface. As it floats out of the bottle it is replaced by water. It can't escape from a bottle held mouth-down. Compare how air escapes out of different containers.

Page 5 The sponge has tiny air holes in it. This is why it is light when dry. When it is immersed, it doesn't go under easily because it is so light. The more air that is squeezed out, the heavier the sponge becomes. The structure of the sponge is interesting because it always springs back to its original shape. This force makes it difficult to squeeze the sponge completely. Compare a synthetic sponge to real ones that lived in the sea.

Page 6 The balloon full of air displaces water. The water exerts a force (called upthrust) to make the balloon float. The balloon goes under when the child's force pushing it down is greater than the upthrust. Try balloons of different sizes; smaller balloons will be easier to push under because they displace less water.

Page 7 The brick has a volume that won't change. As the brick is lowered into the water it displaces, or pushes out of the way, an equal volume of water. For the same reason, the water-level would rise in a half-full tank. The brick is heavier than the same volume of water (i.e. denser) and will sink in water.

Page 8 Some objects float. This is because they are made of a material less dense than water. Children may notice that most floaters feel 'light'.

Page 9 Some materials will sink. They sink because, like the brick, they are denser than water. Even without understanding the concept of density, children can gain useful experience by handling and comparing different materials.

Things look different through water because the rays of light bend as they enter or leave the water. This effect changes what we see. It is most marked in a curved container like a jam jar.

Page 10 Cork floats and plasticine sinks. Corks with sails will roll over in the water because of the shape of the cork and the weight of the sail. By attaching a plasticine weight with a matchstick, the cork boat is given ballast. This lowers the centre of gravity and makes the cork a more stable structure.

Page 11 Plasticine boats can be tricky for small hands to make. Warming and rolling out the plasticine first makes it easier. To float well, the boat needs to have a density less than water. It is this principle that makes all boats float, even when they are made out of metal. If children's first attempts don't work, get them to roll the plasticine thinner and make the sides higher.

Page 12 Mixing the primary-coloured paints makes new colours: blue and red make purple; red and yellow make orange; blue and yellow make green. We see colourful things because light bounces off them and enters our eyes.

Page 13 This activity introduces the idea that sounds can be made artificially. You can also ask children to describe what water sounds like in different situations – such as in a running stream or when it rains. Children can make their own sound effects.

Page 14 All animals and plants need water to grow. So we need water to grow crops for food as well as to keep our bodies working. Children can find out what else we need to make us grow. They can tell you what else they use water for.

Page 15 Do not let children use hot water without direct supervision. Never use boiling water in activities with children. Feeling the difference between hot and cold is easy, but it is more difficult to use a thermometer to measure temperature. This is a skill that takes practice, but for young children it is more important to learn that temperature is measured on a relative scale – high temperatures being hot and low ones cold. Show children how to read a thermometer scale.

Page 16 This activity can familiarize children with the concept of an amount of water having a fixed volume whatever its shape. The different bottles can hold varying volumes of water, i.e., they have different capacities.

Page 17 We use water all the time. From this activity, children can go on to find out what happens to our dirty water. They are also introduced to the method of filtering. Repeated filtering will make the water cleaner, as would filtering through kitchen paper instead of stones to remove the finest dirt.

Pages 18 and 19 Water reacts chemically with other substances. Rust, or iron oxide, is one of the most widely-found examples of such a reaction. This activity shows how things change even if we can't see it happening. It introduces the idea of chemical reactions. Most other metals don't react easily with water and oxygen, but copper wire could be investigated as an exception to this.

Glossary of Words

Filter   Something that will clean water by straining the bits out of it.

Mustard   A small plant that we often eat with cress.

Pebbly   Made up of small, round stones.

Rust   The red stuff on iron that has been wet.

Seeds   The small parts of a plant that will later grow into the same kind of plant.

Solid   Hard, with a fixed shape.

Sound effects   Noises we make to sound like something else.

Surface   The flat top or outside of something.

Temperature   How hot or cold something is.

Testing   Finding out about something.

Thermometer   An instrument for measuring temperature.

Weights   Heavy objects.

Picture Acknowledgements

All photographs are from the **Wayland Picture Library**. The publishers would like to thank all the children, parents and teachers from East Sussex who helped in the making of this book. Artwork illustrations by John Astrop (Sun Studios).

Finding Out More

Series of books that include other topics looked at in the activities in this book:

Material World (Wayland)
My First Science Book (Dorling Kindersley)
Starting Science (Wayland)
Take One (Simon & Schuster)
Thinkabout (Franklin Watts)
Ways to . . . (Franklin Watts)
What's Inside? (Dorling Kindersley)

Resources for teachers:

Materials and Floating by Michael Coyle and Irene Finch (BBC Education). This is part of a video in-service training pack.

Schemes for teaching science topics at this level:

Collins Primary Science by L Howe (Collins, 1990)
Collins Primary Technology by E Chadwick (Collins, 1990)
Nelson Science Key Stage 1 by S Hopkins and A Hunter (Nelson, 1990)

Books for reading and further topic work on water:

Floating and Sinking by Henry Pluckrose (Franklin Watts, 1990)
Rain to Dams – Projects with Water by B Taylor (Gloucester Press, 1990)
Science with Water by Helen Edom (Usborne, 1990)
Water by Hilary Devonshire (Franklin Watts, 1991)
Water by Harriet Hains (Harper Collins, 1989)
Water by Su Swallow (Franklin Watts, 1990)
Water by Brenda Walpole (A & C Black, 1988)
Water in the Home by Martin Thorn, Peter Greenland and Andy Moreland (Macmillan Educational, 1983)

Index